A Science I CAN READ Book

Barn Owl

by Phyllis Flower

Pictures by Cherryl Pape

Harper & Row, Publishers
New York, Hagerstown, San Francisco, London

FIRST EDITION

Library of Congress Cataloging in Publication Data
Flower, Phyllis.
  Barn owl.

  (A Science I can read book)
  1. Barn owl—Juvenile literature.   I. Pape,
Cherryl.   II. Title.
QL696.S85F57 1978   598.9′7   76-58686
ISBN 0-06-021919-X
ISBN 0-06-021921-1 lib. bdg.

Barn Owl

High in the corner of the barn,

the barn owl sits and waits.

She has been sitting on her eggs

for nearly a month.

Sometimes during the day
her mate sits beside her.
When she is hungry,
he brings her food.

At last she feels something move

beneath her.

She stands up

and looks down at her eggs.

They are white and oval,

smaller than hens' eggs.

Last night there were five.

But now there are four.

Next to them

she sees a small white mound.

The barn owl bobs her head

up and down.

She looks at her new baby.

He has tiny white feathers called down.

They are wet now.

But they will dry soon

and become fluffy.

His face is heart-shaped

like his mother's.

His eyes are closed.

His beak is curved.

On the end of his beak

is a special tooth, an egg tooth.

The owlet used it

to break open his shell.

It will fall off soon,

for he no longer needs it.

His ears are openings in his head,

hidden under feathers.

He has four strong toes on each foot.

On the end of each toe

is a sharp hook.

It is called a talon.

Someday he will use his talons

for hunting.

One talon has a very rough edge.

He will use it

to comb his feathers.

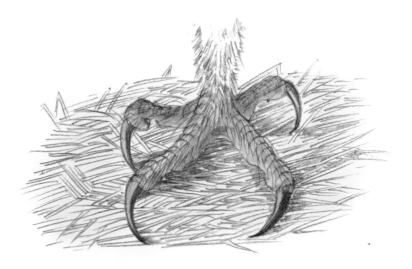

Now the owlet is tired.

Breaking open his shell

was hard work.

He needs to rest.

So he cuddles

under his mother's feathers

and sleeps.

When he wakes up,

he is hungry.

He is ready for the food

his father brings him.

The owlet has a big appetite.

He spends his time

sleeping and eating.

In two days another egg hatches.

The owlet has a brother.

Soon all the eggs have hatched.

When he is about a week old,

the owlet's eyes open.

They are large and round

and dark brown.

He can see well at night with them.

But he can see only straight ahead.

He cannot move his eyes

up or down.

He cannot move them

from side to side.

He has to turn his whole head

to look to the side.

He can turn his head
all the way around
and look behind him.

19

Now he sees his parents
for the first time.
His mother is a little larger
than his father.
Each has a white face and chest.

20

Now the owlet is covered

with short, woolly feathers.

The five baby owls are growing larger.

And they need more food.

The mother owl goes with her mate

to find enough food.

They hunt at night for rats and mice,

small birds,

moths and other insects.

They fly silently.

They can hear a mouse

running over the ground.

They can see a beetle

crawling out from under a rock.

When they find a mouse or rat,

they swoop down on it.

They kill it with their sharp talons.

Then they carry it to the nest.

The babies are waiting for them

with open mouths.

They are always hungry.

The owlet is the oldest
and strongest.
He fights to get fed first.
The others have a turn
after he has been fed.

The owls do not chew their food.

They swallow it whole.

Then they spit up the bones, fur,

and feathers in little bundles.

These bundles are called pellets.

One night the mother owl

goes out hunting with her mate.

And danger enters the barn.

Two yellow eyes.

A dark shadow

with a waving tail.

A cat!

The owlets sway back and forth.

They open their beaks

and make a hissing sound.

The cat has climbed to a rafter

just below the owls' nest.

30

He creeps closer.

The owlets do not scare him.

He creeps closer and closer.

He is about to spring

when the mother barn owl returns.

Zoom!

She swoops toward him

and strikes him with her talons.

The cat yowls.

He tries to jump away,

and falls to the ground.

Quickly he runs out the door.

The mother owl returns

to her family.

The owlets are safe.

34

The owlet is two months old now.

He is as large as his father.

His feathers are smooth and sleek,

white and golden brown.

It is time for him

to learn to fly.

He tries flapping his wings.

He practices for several days.

Then he looks down.

It is a long way to the ground.

The hayloft is closer.

He bobs his head up and down.

At last he spreads his wings
and takes off.
When he flutters his wings,
he comes down. He lands safely
in the hayloft.

One by one, his brothers

follow his example.

At first the young owls practice

flying around the barn.

One morning the owlet

flies near the barn door.

There is a strange noise outside.

The owlet hears it.

He spreads his wings.

He wants to fly to the rafter.

But it is a long way up.

He does not fly high enough.

He lands on the barn floor.

He tries again.

The mother owl

has heard the noise, too.

She flies to the barn door.

The noise comes closer.

It is the voice of a man.

The mother owl tries

to scare him away.

She sits on the ground

and spreads her wings wide.

She hisses.

And she sways from side to side.

She looks very fierce.

But the man does not see her.

He does not come into the barn.

The owlet has flown to the rafter.

He is safe now.

In a short time

the owlets have learned to fly.

But they cannot feed themselves.

When they are hungry,

they call loudly to their parents.

Sometimes the mother owl and her mate

cannot find enough food for them.

It is time for them

to learn to hunt.

The owlet goes out at night
like his father and mother.
He flies silently.
He watches the ground.
He listens for every sound.

There is a rustling noise.

He dives down.

But he finds nothing.

He lands on dry leaves.

Then one night he hears a squeak.

He zooms down, and lands

on something soft and squirmy.

A field mouse!

It is the first meal

he has caught for himself.

A few nights later

the young owl is sitting in a tree.

His brother is out hunting.

He sees him catch a mouse.

His brother carries it to a tree.

Suddenly,

a shadow swoops through the sky.

It plucks his brother from the tree

and carries him off to the forest.

It is the great horned owl,

and it eats other owls.

Now the days are growing cooler.

The leaves turn yellow and red.

The young owl wanders farther

and farther from the barn.

He can feed himself now.

He is old enough to leave his parents.

He finds a place

where hunting is good.

He stays there all winter.

During the day

he sleeps in different places—

on the branch of a tree,

or under the roof of an empty house.

After dark he looks for food.

A cold wind blows.

The ground freezes
and snow comes.

Little animals hide in their holes.

In winter it is hard to find food.

Sometimes the young owl

must hunt by day

to keep his stomach filled.

Many days pass.

The sunlight grows brighter.

The snow begins to melt.

Winter is nearly over.

One chilly night

the young owl is ready to go hunting.

He calls out the way he often does.

Tonight a soft hooting call

answers him.

He hoots once more.

Again there is an answer.

He follows the sound

to the maple tree.

There he finds a female barn owl.

He is excited.

He flutters his wings.

He circles her several times.

Then he flies off.

In a few minutes he returns

with a mouse in his beak.

He drops it in front of her.

She takes the food.

That means she has accepted him

as her mate.

The young owl sits next to her.

They twitter and snap beaks.

Together they sway

from side to side.

They sit together

and sleep in the daytime.

At night they hunt.

60

Before long his mate leads him

to a dead tree.

There is a large hole in it.

She sits inside the hole.

This is where she will lay her eggs.

This is where he will bring food

to their babies

just like his father before him.

The young owl and his mate

may stay together all their lives.

They may live for fifteen years

or even longer.

AUTHOR'S NOTE

Many barn owls die young. Some die because they cannot find enough food. Some are killed by people. People are their worst enemy, because they often put poison out for rats and mice. Owls feed on these animals and die from the poison.

J
598 F
FLOWER
    BARN OWL

38820

4.95